FOR THE
WRITER IN YOU

Vincent J. Sachar

SPECIAL THANKS

To my wife, Gwen, for her encouragement, collaboration, and for providing the first read of everything I write.

Table of Contents

Chapter One

THE BEGINNING

How It Began

It is never too late to be what you might have been.
—George Eliot

My credentials for writing this book are rather simple—*I am you.* I am one of the many with a passion for writing, a desire to produce published works, and a willingness to sacrifice to continue to do something I really love. There are many of us who have this desire to enter a world that we've never been in before—the noble profession of an author. And before we are through with our time together, we'll discuss that nobility.

This book is for anyone and everyone who aspires to be a writer and have their works published. In addition to exploring some fundamental aspects of creative writing, we will also discuss the incredible options that now exist when it comes to publishing—options that, not all that long ago, were non-existent.

With the rise of eBooks and self-publishing, there is a revolution in the world of books that is unprecedented in history. The system whereby publishers controlled the printing presses, the retail distribution of books, and the know-how needed to publish is no longer a credible picture of the entire publishing landscape. Today, authors have the viable option to self-publish and get their book faster to market, at lower expenses, while maintaining greater creative control and acquiring better royalties.

There may be some people who enjoy drafting *Query Letters*, searching for literary agents who might be interested in an author's work, squeezing a three-hundred-page book into a one-page *Synopsis*, and waiting for months or, perhaps, forever, since there will often be no response at all to hear back. That is still the standard process to have your work on the path of acceptance by some big-name publisher. The only modernization to that process is that most literary agents will accept a submission via email. And, the truth is that most of us will do all that because it's what we are required to do. But, it is a tedious and somewhat painful process.

Now don't get me wrong. Traditional publishing does offer some advantages. But, it is no longer the *only* option available to an author and may not always be the best option. Today, a writer can rapidly get his or her product directly into the hands of those whose opinions carry, by far, the greatest significance and value—the readers.

In the section on publishing, we will address both approaches. The important thing for a writer to know is that the playing field to become published is much more balanced and competitive than ever before in the history of books.

My presentation here will often be from the perspective of fiction writing, but, if you are a non-fiction writer, don't fret. Some of the creative writing aspects apply to you as well and the publishing section does not differentiate between fiction and non-fiction.

My goal in writing this is to encourage you to reach out and fulfill your dreams. I'm doing that right now and, as I stated already, I'm just like you. If I can do this, you can do it.

To date, my published works include novels, novellas, and short-stories and I'm still actively writing and creating. I've conducted book events at libraries, bookstores, book clubs, and other unique venues. I've been a panel member at international book conventions and have spoken at universities, colleges, high schools, and even at an elementary school. I've conducted radio interviews, internet website interviews, and participated in blogs. And in so many respects, I am just beginning. Oh, and did I mention that I wrote and published my first two novels while employed full time in a highly-responsible position as a managing director of a global consulting firm? After several years of writing, I am now a "hybrid author," which means I do have a traditional publisher, but I also self-publish.

I say these things not, in any way, to tout myself. Rather, I want you to know that, yes, there are challenges and being an author is not for the half-hearted, but you can do and accomplish far more than you may honestly realize—if you genuinely have a heart to do it. You have to be willing to stick with it and refuse to quit. Perseverance is one of the attributes of a successful writer. You are the one who controls that willingness to press forward.

I will speak about the journey I am on as a published author. I will talk about what it means to be a writer, some key points related to the art of creative writing, completing a book from cover-to-cover, and publishing options. It's time to stop telling yourself you can't and, if you haven't begun, start writing. It is common for a potential author to fear that they do not possess the talent to write something that others would enjoy reading. My advice to them is that they focus on writing for themselves. Write because you love doing it. Just let your creativity flow. You'll soon find that fearing that you lack talent may be the least thing that a writer should worry about.

Some writers have a fear of rejection. Okay, so let's put that one on the table right now. If a fear of rejection stops you from writing, then you might as well put down the pen and find something else to do in your life. Writing and rejection do go hand-in-hand. All authors, even the very best, experience rejection. And the crazy thing is that rejection by literary agents and publishers often says absolutely nothing about your writing skills. Agents and publishers are simply interested in something they believe they can sell at that particular time. Many highly-successful authors had their writings rejected. The list seems endless and the names of these authors are shocking.

I have a perspective on rejection that I cling to and that has allowed me to remain somewhat balanced. Over the years, my children have introduced a variety of singers and songs to me. I loved some. In fact, I placed them in my iTunes library. Others just didn't grab me the same way. None of that really has anything to say about the musicians. It simply helps to define me—my likes, my dislikes, my preferences. We can say the same for artwork or movies. If I look at a painting hanging in an art museum and tell you that I don't like it, does that establish that the painting is not good? Of course, not. In fact, it tells you very little about the painting and more about me. Some people walk out of a movie theater raving over the flick they just sat through. Others may tell you not to bother going to see it.

So, it is with writing. If someone doesn't like something I've written, it might simply be a matter of taste. But, if they reject it because it is poorly written, grammatically sloppy, too hard to understand, or just plain boring, that is my fault. A writer must learn when to take rejection to heart and heed its message and when to recognize different people have differing tastes. Focus on being the best writer you can be and let things proceed from there.

If you haven't started, make the decision to begin. If you have begun, purpose to continue on. It's kind of like a step-by-step trek. I remember the first time someone said to me that they can write, but could not imagine writing an entire book. My response was that I never write an "entire book." I write a book chapter-by-chapter, constructing something that will fit together and, in the end, be a complete product. Like fitting building blocks together, I write a piece of a book, then another piece, then another, and when I'm finished—*voila*—I've got a "whole book." Step-by-step, chapter-by-chapter, you can get there. Reflect with me on this. A page generally consists of about 300 words. A chapter can be as long or short as you reasonably want it to be. My chapters are usually in the range of 1,500 words. That's five pages. Or if your chapters are, say, 1,000 words, that's three-and-a-third pages. See your project in segments or pieces and don't let the entire project overwhelm you.

Start the journey.

◈◈◈

I am an attorney by profession. I earned my Juris Doctor at St. John's Law School in New York. My legal career primarily consisted of in-house corporate legal work, including a position as the youngest Vice President, General Counsel, Corporate Secretary within my industry in the nation. Recently, I retired from my position as a managing director in the legal division of a global consulting company and am now writing full time. People often ask when did I first become a writer. Hah! To be perfectly honest, I've been a writer all my life. Okay, let me explain that more clearly. No, I've not been a published author throughout my life. I didn't write novels early on. But, I've always been a writer in my heart. Writing has always had some place in my life, always.

My wife, Gwen, and I were recently going through some boxes we had put away and we found a poem I wrote when I was eight-years-old. I recall writing stories throughout elementary school. When President John F. Kennedy was assassinated, I wrote a poem. I kept a journal throughout the years. Writing was always something rooted deep within me. Many of you reading this now will know exactly what I'm talking about. Being a writer does not necessarily begin the day you begin writing your first manuscript. It's something that has existed within you well before that time.

I named my author website *Yborn Creations*, based upon Mark Twain's quote: "The two most important days in your life are the day you are born and the day you find out why." I call them "yborns." They have always had a place within you. You could never shake loose from them. Writing is my yborn. Perhaps, it is yours, also.

There's an ancient Chinese proverb that states: "The best time to plant a tree was twenty years ago. The next best time is now." When it comes to writing a novel, I missed my "twenty-years-ago." In recent years, I found my "now."

7

Chapter Two

WRITING

S o, you want to write? You want to be an author? Before we talk about some specific writing techniques and the world of publishing, let's talk.

SOME THINGS ABOUT WRITING:

- Writing is a Lonely Profession
- The Most Significant Part is in the Verb
- Writing is an Ongoing Journey
- There's a Power in Writing

Writing Is a Lonely Profession

Many people hear voices when no one is there. Some of them are called mad and are shut up in rooms where they stare at the walls all day. Others are called writers and they do pretty much the same thing.

—Margaret Chittenden

Despite the obvious humor associated with it, there's a strong element of truth in that quote. Think about it. Writing is a lonely profession because writing itself is an incredibly solitary act. You spend hours alone writing something that initially exists only within your own head. While you're writing, you find yourself engaged in a myriad of conversations and discussions. But, they're all within your mind—no one else's. In fact, no one else is involved in that initial phase of your work. Hey, does that mean I'm really only talking to myself? Well... uh... in a sense, yes. But, that's okay because the characters, the story line, the dialogue you generate between people become very real to you.

If you're writing fiction, for example, you make up stories that never existed before. It is your story. No one else can write it, because no one else knows it. You alone are initially responsible for the storyline, its flow, twists in the plot, and whether you have ultimately provided closure on every open-ended question or issue. The burden of writing something that a reader will finish and identify as a "good read" and worth the investment of their time is on us.

When we create fictitious characters, we describe how they look, how they speak, and reveal their character traits to our readers. Then, we have those characters engage in conversations with each other. Yikes! Fictitious characters who engage in fictitious activities and have fictitious conversations with other fictitious characters that we've also created. And within a relatively short time, these characters are alive and real to us. Sound a bit strange or bizarre? It gets worse. Our goal as writers is to get the reader to feel as we do.

One of the most rewarding aspects of being a writer is meeting with a book club or receiving feedback from a reader and listening to them refer to your characters as people who are real to them.

> *Which of us has not felt that the character we are reading in the printed page is more real than the person standing beside us? —Cornelia Funke.*

You may have others collaborate with you, provide an initial read, edit your work, even critique it. But let's be clear. The actual task of writing belongs to you and you alone. And that can definitely create a somewhat cloistered feeling, no matter how much you enjoy writing. And as you write, you alone are initially judging your work, uncertain just how well it will be received by others.

Defining writing as a lonely profession does not necessarily carry a negative connotation. We are talking more about the fact that the responsibility is yours and you must have the discipline to get your work done. But anything negative is greatly offset by the euphoria writers often experience when those creative juices are flowing and blank pages become filled with life.

But, if you're going to be a writer, you will spend countless hours alone. It just goes with the territory.

The Most Significant Part Is in the Verb

If you want to be a writer you must do two things above all others: read a lot and write a lot.

—Stephen King

I cannot tell you how many people I know who, when they heard I had written a book, told me they've always intended to write one, also. But that's just it. You don't become a writer by dreaming of becoming one, desiring to become one, intending to become one, talking about becoming one, nor even by planning to one day become one. Writers primarily do one thing—*they write*. And that requires a discipline, a doing it, even if, at times, you're not particularly in the mood to do so. That's no different than many things in life, whether it be studying to earn a degree or learning a trade or even becoming proficient in a sport. Let's face it.

Some days the words will flow like rivers of sparkling water. On other days, you may feel as if you are swimming in mud. That's okay. You can always go back and fine tune your words. Just get going. Write them down. Listen, you can always make something out of something, but you can't make something out of nothing. Huh? What I'm saying is once you have written something, you've got at least a basis to work from. You can edit, correct, improve, but, at least, you have a starting point.

And keep reminding yourself that writing is a *verb,* an action word, a doing of something.

In Stephen King's quote at the beginning of this section, he cites reading as a major prerequisite to becoming a writer. When you read, whether you do so consciously or unconsciously, you expose yourself to the art of writing.

If you don't feel you're quite ready to launch your first novel, write by keeping a journal. You can also practice a bit by doing a few exercises. I have challenged people at a book event or students in schools to simply create a fictitious character. Describe that character's appearance, how he or she speaks, how they dress, their background, where they are from, how educated they are. Determine what some of your character's strong points are. What do they fear? What are their goals or desires?

Once you start the process, you'll quickly realize how much you can do in identifying your character. Then, create another character. Afterwards, have your characters speak to each other. Sound difficult? Little girls and boys do some of this at an early age when playing with their action figures, dolls, stuffed animals, and other toys.

The point is that to become a writer, you must do what a writer does. Improving on your skills comes later. The first step is to *write*.

Writing Is an Ongoing Journey

If I waited for perfection, I would never write a word.

—Margaret Atwood

There is no reason to wait until you become an expert writer before you begin, because none of us ever will completely master the art of writing. The more we learn, the more we realize we don't know. But, that's not discouraging. It's comforting to know that we always have room to grow, always can take on new and exciting challenges, always can get better over time.

You do need to take time to get grounded in the fundamentals of grammar, punctuation, and certain basic aspects of writing. But, in truth, just when you learn something new, you realize there is so much more that lies ahead.

I first discovered this years ago. I recall reading a book by a well-known author. I thoroughly enjoyed it and, as we are prone to do, I started to seek out other books by that same author. I was reading some of that author's earliest novels. His publisher re-published some, following his rise to fame. That's when I saw it. The earlier books were still enjoyable, still great stories, but there was something deeper, something more polished and mature in the author's more recent published works. I saw it in the descriptions of people, places, and events. I saw it in the dialogue. I remember when the discovery first hit me that this author has grown over time.

I already look at something I first wrote and see where I would do things differently and better today. But, hold on! Where isn't that true? The outstanding rookie athlete, the college athlete who becomes a professional, or people, even people who are gifted and exceptionally skilled, all grow. So, do we as writers. Start now and grow as you continue to write.

And the most encouraging aspect of this is that you don't have to reinvent the wheel or simply hope to learn something by some strange method of supernatural osmosis. The Internet is filled with information related to writing and writing techniques. Or you can acquire an inexpensive book on writing by other authors that will teach you things you didn't know and take you to places where you've never been. Or simply follow the advice of someone like Mark Twain who says, "Writing is easy. All you have to do is cross out the wrong words." Okay, so it may not be that simple, but the point remains. There are so many available resources to assist you on your journey to becoming a better writer.

My first published works are all in the third person point of view. I honestly wondered if I could ever write anything in the first person. Then, one day, I wrote an anecdotal account that covered the time when I journeyed as a seventeen-year-old from New York to New Orleans to attend college and ended up meeting my wife-to-be in Cajun country. It is entitled, *Cajun Culture Shock,* and I wrote it entirely in the first person. Since then, I've written two novellas in the first person. I found that I was entirely comfortable doing so and genuinely enjoyed it.

Start writing and, in time, you leap over hurdles you originally thought were impossible to conquer.

There's a Power in Writing

> *Words can be like x-rays if you use them properly—they'll go through anything. You read and you're pierced.*

> —Aldous Huxley

> *If a nation loses its storytellers, it loses its childhood.*

> —Peter Handke

A writer has the power to make a reader laugh, cry, ponder, question, learn, and enjoy—all arising from the words he or she puts together. That's really powerful stuff right there.

> *All words are pegs to hang ideas on.*

> —Henry Ward Beecher.

Throughout history, the written word has changed the very world we live in. Disregarding for the moment major religious writings, just consider, "We hold these truths to be self-evident that all men are created equal, that they are endowed by their Creator with certain unalienable Rights, that among these are Life, Liberty and the pursuit of Happiness." And these words penned by Thomas Jefferson in the Declaration of Independence not only launched the initial phase of a people seeking liberty from an oppressive nation, they are alive today reminding us of our responsibilities whenever specific peoples are found to be lacking in their personal rights and liberty.

When President Abraham Lincoln, while engulfed in the Civil War, met Harriet Beecher Stowe, the author of *Uncle Tom's Cabin,* he purportedly greeted her saying, "So you're the little woman who wrote the book that started this great war."

There's power in writing—a good power—and this includes the ability to permit readers to find a haven or sanctuary that provides them with a respite from their daily hurts, problems, and pressures.

> *I love books. I love that moment when you open one and sink into it you can escape from the world*

—Elizabeth Scott

Chapter Three

WRITERS

SOME THINGS ABOUT AN AUTHOR:

You must want to enough. Enough to take all the rejections, enough to pay the price of disappointment and discouragement.

—Phyllis Whitney

W riting is no different than any other pursuit in life. You've got to want it and love what you are doing. It requires a discipline and a perseverance that can only come from you.

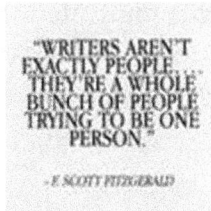

"WRITERS AREN'T EXACTLY PEOPLE... THEY'RE A WHOLE BUNCH OF PEOPLE TRYING TO BE ONE PERSON."

- F. SCOTT FITZGERALD

WHAT'S WHAT?

Let's take a moment to identify the various forms of writing that you may engage in. The word numbers may vary a bit depending upon where you look, but the ones provided here are certainly good enough to rely upon.

Short Story – 3,500 – 7,500 words Used to describe a single event, episode, or tale of one character. Meant to be read in a single sitting.

Novelette – 7,500 – 17,500 words Longer than a short story, but shorter than a novella, the term is rarely used today. A novellete is a narrative fictional prose that once referred to a story that was romantic or sentimental in character. Today they are rarely published singly.

Novella – 17,000 – 40,000 words Sometimes referred to as a long short story or a short novel. Can involve more than one sub-plot, twists, and characters. (Some famous novellas: "A Christmas Carol" – Charles Dickens; "Strange Case of Dr Jekyll and Mr Hyde" – Robert Louis Stevenson; "Of Mice and Men" – John Steinbeck; "The Old Man and the Sea" – Ernest Hemingway; "Animal Farm" – George Orwell.)

Novel – 40,000+ words Often involves multiple major characters, sub-plots, points of view, and twists. The word counts will vary depending upon the particular genre of the book. Different genres have different word count requirements. Generally, a novel could be said to be one that contains 80,000 to 120,000 word. Romance novels are often shorter. Fantasy, horror, and science fiction books often have greater length. It depends upon the font you are using, but, in general, 250-300 words per page is a common calculation to determine the number of pages of your book.

Questions Every Writer Gets Asked

1. Where do you get your ideas?

I laughed aloud when Stephen King mentioned in his book, *On Writing*, that this is the one question that he and other writers never ask each other because "none of us know." Simply stated, we often respond that our ideas come from life all around us.

Truth is, I never get a complete idea. I get a seed, a "what if" that then germinates within my mind and begins to form a story. And even then, the story grows once I begin writing. I authored a trilogy of books, which I commonly refer to as the *Nowhere Trilogy*. In the first book, *The Nowhere Man*, my protagonist, Kent Taylor, is a decorated Navy SEAL who ends up stripped of all that he loves and lives for. Taylor is gravely injured and incarcerated in a foreign prison overseas while on a covert mission. Meanwhile, his wife, an assistant district attorney in New York, inadvertently uncovers a major government scandal.

In order to silence her, Taylor's wife is murdered along with his young son, and his in-laws. Taylor, back in the US, seeks out those responsible for the deaths of his loved ones and becomes an assassin. He is so talented and elusive that the media dubs him *The Ghost Assassin.* The second book in the series, *Nowhere Out,* focuses on Taylor some fourteen years later. He's living in total seclusion as the only person on earth who knows his true identity. The third book, *Nowhere On Earth,* picks up about a year-and-a-half afterwards.

Each book has its own series of suspense, thrills, and adventures, but I want you to hear the key point in this discussion. Three books replete with all the action, drama, and excitement, filled with new and some returning characters, all were birthed from a single seed that entered my mind. And that seed actually related to book two.

What if there was a man living in total seclusion, who is hidden away from the world he lives in? He may go days, weeks, even months without ever talking with another person. And he is the only person in the world who knows his true identity. There's something hidden deeply in his past—something dark. But, the man is not some evil, sinister character. Rather, he's a man of good character who was unjustly betrayed and stripped of everything he loved and valued.

That was my seed. Then, questions sprang up in my mind. What and who is he hiding from? Something dark occurred in his past. Perhaps, he committed a series of murders but is not an evil man. So, what prompted him? What kind of betrayal? Perhaps, some people in the very government for which he risked his life countless times are behind the murders of his loved ones. I needed to make the man formidable—here's where the Navy SEAL identity came from.

Anyway, you get the picture. One seed. I let it germinate and three books were birthed from it. In a sense, that's how writers get our ideas for books. There are seeds, ideas for books, all around us. We simply need to train ourselves to take the time to look for them.

2. How do you deal with Writer's Block?

I've heard writer's block defined as "when your imaginary friends stop speaking to you." There may be a lot of truth in that.

If I feel a bit stifled in an existing project, it may be because I am striving to solve everything at once, make everything perfect now when there's really no need to do so. At times such as this, I go back through what I've already written, let the story flow in my mind again, and, invariably, new ideas surface. Another way in which I have responded when I seem to be sluggish is to skip ahead in my writing to a scene that I know I will include and let the connecting chapters flow when they are ready.

And then, there are times when I am not all that enamored with a section of the book I am writing, but I move forward anyway. I can always go back later and refine and edit what I wrote. It is easier to take something and improve it than to stare at a blank page and ponder what I need to put there to fill it.

Another thing I do is to have more than one project going concurrently. One is my primary project. The other is a future work and may be a novella or a short story. This simply gives me something else I can turn to on a day or at a time when my primary project seems to be in a bit of a rut or I am somewhat limited in my focus and my time.

On the subject of what should I write next, I keep a list of potential books that pop into my head at times. They may never get written or, as I mentioned earlier, something may be a seed that begins to germinate and come to life.

Keep a journal. Jot down ideas as they come to you. Jot down names, places, thoughts, sentences that come to mind from time to time. Once again, you can always look back later and see what, if anything, seems to have life.

Remember, there are potential stories around us every day as we walk through life itself. Look for them.

3. Have you ever based a book character on a person you actually know?

Most of us would likely say we have never based a character upon a real person, but, let's face it, we pick up personality characteristics, nuances, manners of speaking, and more from people all around us. Most writers are people watchers and observers of life itself. We notice how people act, react, speak, and dress. We hear dialects, foreign languages, accents from people for whom English is not their first or primary language. We hear colloquialism, slang, and a variety of expressions simply by being around people on the job or in public places. We see people when they are happy, sad, angry, shocked, startled, surprised, comical, or in love. Pieces of the characters we create are around us every day, even when we are not focused on any one person.

I read somewhere that Charles Dickens used to listen closely to people's names and make a note of anything unique he might later choose to use. The story may be apocryphal, but I read somewhere that Dickens met a man at a party. Upon hearing the man's name. Dickens told him his name would be known throughout the world before the year's end. The man was said to be named, "Doctor Marley."

Incidentally, when people ask if we have ever based a character on someone we actually know, we should ask readers which character in our books do they believe most resembles themselves. Odds are they won't choose the villain.

4. Do you outline your novels or just write as you go?

People often wonder how we are able to write an entire novel with its storyline, plot diversions, and twists. Little do they know that many authors finish writing something and ask the same question. Yes, some are "plotters" and some are "pantsers."

"Plotters" spend a great deal of time before writing. They plan and outline what they intend to write. The extent of their planning may be extremely detailed. Some plotters identify and describe in detail every character they intend to include in their book and every scene.

"Pantsers," as the word implies, write "by the seat of their pants." They begin with a theme, an idea, a general thrust or direction, and then create as they write.

Even so, all writers do end up looking at a finished product with a certain amount of "Man, where in the world did that come from?".

Everything I have ever written has scenes, characters, plot twists, and more that I did not have in mind when I first began writing it.

And, I personally believe that if an author outlined everything they were going to write in a book, fiction or non-fiction, the book would still have portions the author did not have in mind when he or she first started writing it.

5. What does it take to become a writer?

An author can rattle off any number of characteristics ranging from a vivid imagination, a discipline, or a command of language. Truth is, a writer must write. It is amazing how many people I know have told me that they have always intended to write a book. A person can outline an entire book, but it is still not written until they sit down and write it. As I stated earlier, we do not become writers by intending to become one, hoping to be one, planning to be one. Writers write—pure and simple.

So, what does it take to become an author whose works others would like to read. Must someone be an expert in language and grammar? The answer is "no." You don't need to have a Ph.D. in English nor be highly-proficient in grammar, punctuation, and spelling. These are things you can constantly learn more about and improve upon and there are plenty of resources available throughout the internet. Yes, a writer should strive to be grounded in the fundamentals of grammar, punctuation, spelling, and vocabulary, so as to be able to complete sentences and communicate clearly to others. But, perhaps, the strongest characteristics of a writer is an unrelenting desire to be one and the discipline required to put the necessary time in to write. Remember, as we said earlier, whatever you intend to write is locked somewhere within your own mind and you alone can unloose it. That requires commitment and discipline.

Chapter Four

PREPARATIONS

One day Alice came to a fork in the road and saw a Cheshire Cat in a tree. "'Which road do I take?" she asked. "Where do you want to go?" was his reply. "I don't know," Alice answered. "Then," said the cat," it doesn't matter, does it?"

—Lewis Carrol

Writing a novel is like driving a car at night. You can only see as far as your headlights, but you can make the whole trip that way."

—E.L. Doctorow

Know Where You're Going

Even if you are not prone to heavily outline your anticipated book, you still need a starting point and a basic idea of where you are going. The time to determine the genre you are writing in and the general theme of your book is before you start. I described writing a novel as a journey. Okay, then, before you begin, you need to decide what your starting point is and what your ending will be.

It's perfectly fine that you don't know every detail, every nuance relating to your story. It's okay that you may create additional characters along the way. You s,hould expect that you'll develop twists, turns, and new developments once you are into your writing---after all, that's part of the creativity you are engaged in when you write. But, you need to know the nature of the journey you are making. You can't decide to drive from Charlotte to New Orleans and end up in Buffalo.

By way of example, in my thriller/suspense novel, *A Life Unappreciated*, I started with the basic theme of creating someone who is already engaged in covert work that, by its very nature, doesn't generate a whole lot of thankfulness from others. Undercover work is, itself, secretive and hidden from the eyes of most others. Then, my goal was to have that person wrongly accused and betrayed, so his lack of appreciation for all he has done is compounded. My protagonist would go through great trials in his efforts to escape capture and prove his innocence, but in the end he would be proven innocent. That was generally my goal, the journey I would put my lead character on. If he was going to be involved in undercover work, of neccesity, I needed to place him in a profession that includes that kind of work. I chose by having my protagonist be a highly-trained special agent. I would not kill him. He would succeed in being proven innocent, but he would be scarred along the way. At least, I knew my journey and had a rough idea of where it would begin and end. The book would be a thriller/suspense novel with elements of mystery intertwined throughout the plot.

In my novel, *Nowhere Out*, my protagonist, Kent Taylor, is hidden away, so secluded from society and the world around him that he is the only person on the planet who knows his true identity. I intended to place him in situations that force him to choose between using his incredible skills to save the lives of innocent others or continue to turn his head and do nothing. His choice would involve the risk of exposure. A woman he meets helps to break down the walls he has built over many years and heighten the pressure he feels in the decisions he must either make or reject.

The book, although it stands completely alone in its plot, is a sequel to my first novel, *The Nowhere Man*, which means that there are certain ekements of Taylor's past and his personality that must remain consistent in this novel.

I believe that even if you sit down and, over the course of time, outline every detail in the book you intend to write, your final product will differ in many aspects from what you outlined. There's no need to know every detail of your book before you start writing. You just need to establish certain key elements and go from there.

There! I know the nature of the book I intend to write, where I will begin and where I'm headed. Now, all I needed was details and my ability to remain consistent with my theme for the novel. I still didn't have all the inner guts, but at least I knew what my journey was going to be.

Who's Your Protagonist?

Once I had a general idea of the nature and theme of my next book, A *Life Unappreciated*, I needed to give some detailed thought to my protagonist. I needed a gender, a name, background, location, description, and key motivation that affects choices my character will make. Is he or she educated? I could go on and on listing personality characteristics and details related to my protagonist and some authors do exactly that. They create a chart that sets forth all kinds of details related to each character, beginning with their protagonist. But, even if you don't do that, you still need to have a solid concept regarding your key character. Remember, as with all characters you create, you must stay consistent with how they speak, act, and react.

When you focus on your lead character and the position that he or she will be placed in, you'll find that you naturally begin to develop their personality more and come up with reasons that explain their motives for choices they've made and will make in your story. I needed my character to be formidable, someone who worked undercover, and someone capable of handling the incredible pressure I would thrust on him. I created a character named Brett Gatlin. His background included the fact that he was an outstanding athlete in high school, a top academic student all the way through his time at the

Vanderbilt University's tier one law school. Then, just when he has graduated with top honors and is being sought by Fortune 500 corporations and some of the best law firms in the nation, Brett's kid brother, a gang member addicted to heroin, is found dead in a Nashville alley—a victim of a gang war. Brett chooses to forego his lucrative offers and become a DEA Special Agent.

In working on the creation of my protagonist, I fulfill another key requirement mentioned in the next chapter, namely, that we must create characters that a reader will care about. No matter how great a story may be, a reader will not continue with it if he or she does not care about your protagonist.

When I first began writing novels, I read somewhere that, in developing the plot of a book, an author needs to follow his or her protagonist. My initial reaction was: Huh? Say what? Am I missing something here? I mean how do I follow someone that I created, someone who does not move, speak, or even exist outside of me?

I have since learned the meaning of that statement. When I create a character, I put that person in situations that, of necessity, generate certain actions, reactions, needs, and concerns. Some things, which are essential to my plot, place my character in situations that require me to get creative and come up with a solution, another action, or reaction.

In my novel, *Nowhere Out*, the third book in a trilogy featuring Kent Taylor, my protagonist is forced to utilize and rely upon his training and experience as a former

Navy SEAL in order to save the lives of people close to him.

Before you begin writing, take some time to reflect upon your protagonist and what he or she is like. Of course, you can also begin developing other key characters, but your first go is to determine who your protagonist will be, what situation he or she will be placed in, what they are seeking, and what they are like.

In my murder mystery, *Murders at Pearl Springs*, I wanted to create a female protagonist and challenge myself to the task of writing from the perspective of the gender opposite to my own. I had to think as a female would, recognize the challenges unique to her gender, strive to create a female character who is believeable, likable, and will generate an interest from my readers. As the first and only female detective in her police department's history, a position for which she beat out several male colleagues, Heather Lance has to deal with gender bias and even some sexual harrasment. My character had to be a female fully capable of handling the demands of a job in law enforcement.

Establish Your Point of View

Before you begin writing, you need to determine whether you will wtrite in the

first person, second person, or third person.

First Person (I, We) --- In this point of view, a character is speaking throughout the book from his or her perspective. In this type of narrative, it is as if we are inside the head of a certain character. The story unfolds only through the eyes of that person. A reader may be drawn in closely as a character speaks directly to the person reading. One major disadvantage to writing in the first person is the fact that everything is limited to what this character knows or even could know. If your character is entering a dark house and someone is hidden in there waiting to attack, that is not something the character knows and can share with a reader.

Second Person (You) --- This is a much rarer point of view utilized by authors of novels. It tells the story by reference to someone able to speak from the perspective limited to a protagonist or lead character, which still limits the knowledge that can be shared.

Third Person (He, She, It, They) --- A much broader perspective as the author is not limited to a single character. Remember, any one character cannot know what other people are thinking or feeling. But, writing in the third person allows an author to share the point of view of a number of characters.

I have written in the first person for a biograpical account of my first year of college (*Cajun Culture Shock*) where I journeyed into New Orleans, met the gitrl I would marry, and was introduced to the Cajun culture in Houma. I also wrote in the first person for *ID:The Man with Two Lives* and *A Twisted Road.* My other writings are in the third person.

Summary List of Things to Consider Before You Start

- Decide what your book will be about. Establish a starting point and an end-goal. Set a theme in mind. Will your novel be dark, light, filled with heavy drama or humor?

- Create your protagonist. Remember that he or she must be someone who a reader can attach to and care about. (HINT: If you create someone that YOU really care about, it will be ingrained in your writing.) In addition to providing such things as your character's physical appearance, personality traits, and general background, what is it that your protagonist is dealing with and must conquer, achieve, or overcome. What's at stake if your lead character fails? Also, start thinking about other key characters, including an antagonist, if needed. (HINT: An antagonist should have something that does attract a reader. You might explain briefly why this person has become what they are—abandoned or abused as a child—without justifying them.)

- Select a set time and place to do your writing. Without discipline, most people fail. Treat your writing as if it were a paid job and not a mere hobby. If it further helps you set goals—a chapter a day, a certain amount of words per day, a page a day (HINT: A page is about 300 words). Daily goals give you a set target and if you keep those goals small, they are attainable and can be expanded over time. You might even set goals for when you would like to complete your book.

- Keep a journal and jot things down that come to mind even when you are not writing. I also rely on the Dropbox App so that I have access on my iPad and iPhone to things I am writing even when I'm not at my computer. When you're in a waiting room for a doctor, dentist, getting the oil changed for your car, or whatever, you can do some writing or creative thinking related to your book.

- Set a goal and remind yourself continually that you will not quit. There's no other way to say it, there's no other way to do it, you just have to develop a mindset that no matter what, you will not quit. No one is interested in the book you almost wrote.

Chapter Five

START THE JOURNEY

There are three rules for writing a novel. Unfortunately, no one knows what they are.

—W. Somerset Maugham

W ell, there really are some rules and we all *kind of know* what they are, but it is also true that creative writing does provide an author with a great deal of freedom and self-expression. Nevertheless, there are some things that every writer should know. Let's talk about them. Before we discuss some specific writing techniques, let's explore those things that constitute a good book.

WRITING A BOOK WORTH READING

INTRODUCTION

It's pretty much impossible to describe a book that everyone loves. The same is true with various forms of art, music, and cinema. People have different tastes and may even have differing reasons why they read fiction. Even so, whether some read because they want to laugh, cry, learn, or because they prefer action or drama, there is one thing in common for all readers. *They want to be entertained.* They want to be able to say when they finish a book that it was worth the time invested in reading it. The book was a "good read."

Fiction authors should set a number one priority of entertaining the reader. Secondarily, a fiction novel might teach or impart knowledge about certain things. If the author can accomplish both, so much the better.

Of course, the reverse is true when we speak about non-fiction books. There, the priority is to teach or impart knowledge. Secondarily, a non-fiction book might also entertain. This might easily explain the popularity of the "For Dummies" books. The books are written to teach or impart knowledge, but, at the same time, they are fun to read and entertaining.

REMEMBER: If a reader doesn't like what I wrote, that may simply be a matter of taste. But, if my writing was confusing to a reader or if my book is boring or shoddy, then I am to blame.

WHAT HELPS MAKE A BOOK A GOOD READ:

CHARACTERS – Some believe that creating characters is the single-most important aspect of novel writing. It certainly is up there with the need to develop a page-turning plot. But, even with an enthralling story, readers will only care what happens next, if they care about the characters at the heart of the action.

Hey, maybe you know someone who goes on and on bragging about everything he's ever supposedly done. They babble, taking forever to make a point, and never let anyone else speak. If so, you would clearly not enjoy being with this person and would try your best to avoid spending time together.

Or maybe you know people who have a list of what's wrong with everything and everyone in the universe— except when it comes to themselves. Spending time with them is like being in a dark, black cloud.

Or what about the person who drones on telling you every minute detail about some movie or television show that you have no interest in.

Well-developed, good, strong characters are the backbone of a good book. They are a *must*. Your protagonist doesn't have to be perfect. In fact, in many instances, it is preferable if he or she is not. *But a reader must be willing to spend some time with the characters you create.* Your characters must be likeable. It doesn't matter that your characters are fictitious. If you want a reader to stay within the pages of your book, they must be reading about characters they like. Let's face it, in life, no one wants to spend time with people they do not enjoy. Give some careful thought to creating your characters. Remember that real people are complicated and have fears, desires, and needs that sometimes conflict. Consider basic traits such as age, gender, height, weight, eye color, and hair color. Then keep adding to the profile. How educated is this character? How does she/he speak? Is this character outgoing or introverted? Happy or unhappy? The choices are yours. Let your creativity flow.

We sometimes have people in our lives because we are related to them or we work together with them. Or, perhaps, we are talking about someone who lives next door, is a coworker, or sits in the same classroom. Okay, so sometimes I'm stuck with the person sitting near me in a waiting room who seems to believe that shouting into a cell phone is the only way the person on the other end of his phone can hear him. These same people also seem to think that everyone else in that room wants to know all the details of their lives. I mean why wouldn't we want to know about their hernia, reasons for hating their mother, or drunken uncle who is also a thief? Anyway, these are instances when we're forced to deal with people who have no other purpose in our lives other than to irritate us and increase our blood pressure levels.

Not so with book characters. Every character in a book ought to be there for a specific purpose. There is something that character wants—something they are after. Bear in mind that with a reader we are not talking about someone forced to stay on a bus, sit in a waiting room, or attending a family function. All a reader has to do is close the book or turn off their reading device and the problem is solved.

Our characters, even though fictitious, are defined by a specific personality and attitude. It defines who they are and what makes them tick. The aspects of their personality may be based upon where are they from, how educated they are, and their life experiences. We may find hints of their personalities in the way they speak or dress. Take the time to look around at people in your everyday life and you'll see how they carry a certain image.

Even our villains need to be well-developed characters. They may be highly-intelligent or even quite charismatic. An author may cite reasons why a villain evolved into what he or she has become or why they feel justified in what they are doing.

In my thriller/suspense novel, *Nowhere Out*, the villain, in addition to being super-talented, is someone who is intelligent and would never be recognized as a paid professional killer by people who encounter him in the daily course of life. His incredible narcissism will prove to be his undoing.

It is important to remember that our characters must be consistent in their actions, reactions, in their speech, and in the way they think. Solid book characters will stir emotions as our readers attach to them. And I can tell you that whenever I hear readers talk about my characters as if they are real people and express a variety of emotions in how they feel about them, I am both humbled and thrilled.

Take a moment and think of successful movies or television programs. As you do, you will invariably find characters that viewers attach themselves to and get to know. The same is true with the characters we create in our writings. So, take the time to create characters who are likeable and dynamic. Make your protagonist good at what he or she does. Put your protagonist in a position where they suffer. Generate sympathy from your readers. Let your readers see your protagonist struggle in whatever it is he or she is battling against. And put everything you can at stake. Readers want to see your lead character beat the odds and win.

Remember: We may have a great storyline, but if our characters do not spur interest or in some manner, inspire a reader, our book will fail.

Some character questions:

Are my characters likeable? Will a reader want to spend time with them? Care about them?

Is my protagonist good at what he/she does?

Are my characters (especially lead characters) charismatic?

Are my characters (especially lead characters) dynamic?

Have I placed my protagonist in a position where he/she is embattled and has something major to lose?

A PAGE-TURNING PLOT - The plot is the storyline of a novel. It's the tale that we weave and the way it evolves. Good books have a plot that flows and moves. A good book requires action to keep the reader's interest. When we talk more about some of the basic writing techniques, we will discuss how the first chapter of a book needs to contain a *hook* that grabs a reader's attention and makes them want to continue reading. But, even after a reader decides to stick with your book, there must be enough action, enough movement, to keep the reader interested. You want your reader to look forward to getting back to your book in between their reading times.

Every chapter beginning should reignite the reader's interest and every chapter ending should generate a desire to move onto the next. When you hear readers saying that they could not put a book down, they're stating the plot kept them engaged.

Your plot should not be so predictable that your reader knows exactly what will happen next. Surprise your readers with some twists and unexpected turns. Cause them to worry about characters they have come to like. I have, at times, placed key characters in situations that even I, at first, was not quite sure how I would be able to get them out of, in a credible manner.

Also, remember a good plot does more than tell a story. It stimulates thought in the reader, evokes emotions, imparts something of value to a reader. Someone once said that a good book continues with a reader even after they have finished reading it.

Another key aspect of the plot is its conclusion. Have you ever watched a drama on television that was exciting and really drew you in until a quick, lame ending spoiled everything?

A writer needs to give serious thought to the conclusion of the story. You need to think ahead about how your story will end. You don't want your conclusion to be a disappointment to your reader. It must be plausible, a natural outcome or flow from the story itself—even if it contains an element of surprise. It is the last taste, the final thought a reader has as they end their time of commitment. An unrealistic, forced, or contrived ending can spoil the taste of the entire book. Just as your first chapter was the hook to convince the reader to stay with your book, the last chapter convinces them that it was worth the investment of their time. It also is the key to spurring a reader on towards your next or other books.

Some plot questions:

> *Is my story consistent? (In the description of* characters, in their mannerisms, in their speech);

> How did the story end? Was the ending contrived, forced, unrealistic? Was the ending disappointing?

> Is my story too predictable? (It's okay for some things in a story to be predictable, but readers also expect to encounter some twists and turns, some unexpected things. Readers like to worry about characters caught in a crisis. Be sure that your reader does not know everything that is about to happen).

Some basic plot questions:

-Why do I care (or not) about this story?

-What is it about the characters (or not) that grabs me?

-How does each scene begin and end?

-How do I feel at the end of the book?

DIALOGUE – One of the areas I have worked strongest on from book-to-book is improving dialogue. That's because dialogue is a key element in any fiction novel. Dialogue is said to be the clearest indicator of an author's writing quality. For every writer, this is an area that demands attention and focus.

As writers, we need to create dialogue that sounds like the way people talk in real life, yet does not. Huh? Okay, I know that sounds a bit fuzzy, but stick with me here for a minute. What I'm saying is real life speech is often boring and meaningless. A conversation might wander all over the place until you find yourself staring like a cross-eyed listener thinking only of how you can escape from this torture. If you can't stand listening to boring people in real life, why in the world do you want to torture yourself dealing with that stuff when you're supposedly reading a book for entertainment?

As writers, we need to find a way to create dialogue that sounds real, but is tailored to fit into our story and meet a desired purpose. Dialogue helps to move the story forward. All dialogue needs to have some purpose behind it. When we write, we should think of speech as connected to some type of activity.

We use fictional dialogue to help reveal story information that will enable a reader to better understand what's going on. But, dialogue should never contain anything that both characters already know.

We also use fictional speech to assist in revealing character. A reader can learn much by the way a character speaks. Dialogue can reveal a person's background, level of education, regionalism, and so much more. The way we mix words together (syntax) might reveal that English is not a character's native language. The use of certain words and phrases might reveal that characters are lawyers, doctors, or, even, thugs.

We use fictional dialogue to set a scene and bring the reader into a setting where things may be dark, spooky, or in an amusement park, a forest, or atop a mountain.

Dialogue also helps set the tone of a book. People in an old western town talk differently than those in a book about King Arthur and his Round Table Knights.

You might also consider gender specific dialogue, recognizing that men and women have basic differences in their speech patterns. Men ask more questions. They want more information and answers. The responses of men are often shorter and more specific. Men pay less attention to detail and speak less emotively than women. They use less metaphors and euphemisms and care less about other people's opinions of what they say. Women give more advice and more freely offer their opinions. A woman generally thinks about what the other person has said, carefully considers it, then reacts. Females are more likely to notice details of places, people, and things around them and include specific details in their dialogue. Women talk more emotionally and persuasively and are more likely to use metaphors and euphemisms. They commonly use phrases like "I think," and "I feel."

One beneficial practice for a writer is to read the dialogue aloud and listen to what they have written. Also, look to see whether your dialogue reveals character, is an alternative to narrative in revealing story info, sets the scene, or provides a tone for your book. Is at least one of these elements in your dialogue? Does your dialogue advance the plot, add energy to your story, draw your reader in? If your dialogue does not contain any of these things, it is useless and serves no worthwhile purpose in your novel.

Some dialogue questions:

Does my dialogue reveal character?

Does it add story info?

Does my dialogue advance the plot of my story?

Does my dialogue ever set the scene?

Does it flow?

VOICE – A writing voice is unique to every writer. It's what makes Hemingway sound like Hemingway and Stephen King sound like Stephen King. It's the way we write, the words we use, the voice that readers listen to when they read that author's book. It is personal and unique to each author, just as our everyday speech helps to identify our personal style. Even so, the goal every writer should have is to make our readers feel as if they are right in the very midst of our characters, involved in all the action and the setting.

> *All good books are alike in that they are truer than if they had really happened. And after you are finished reading one, you will feel that all that happened to you and afterwards it belongs to you: the good and the bad, the ecstasy, the remorse and sorrow, the people and places and how the weather was. If you can get so that you can give that to people, then you are a writer.*
>
> —Ernest Hemingway

Perhaps, the best way to define voice is to say that each of us as writers should be true to ourselves. We may glean from other authors, but our voice should be our own. Our goal should never be to mimic another author. People who know me well say that they often can hear me in my writings.

Think about it. A writer's voice is the very thing that makes the author unique. Voice consists of the words we choose to use, the flow of our sentences, the length of our chapters, our use of punctuation, the amount of dialogue in our books, the amount of description, and more. When we place ourselves into the words we write and generate a sense that a character is an actual person conveying the writer's message, that is a writer's voice. And if a writer's voice is an expression of the writer on a page, then our writing must be an honest, unadulterated expression of our hopes, dreams, thoughts, passions, beliefs, and fears contained in every word that we write.

Be yourself.

Some voice questions:

Is my writing my own expression?

Is my voice consistent with the primary purpose of a non-fiction book (to teach or explain)? A fiction novel (to entertain)?

Did I try to mimic another author or stay true to my own unique writing voice?

THEME – A good book should mean something or, at the very least, cause a reader to ponder about something in a new way. The Oxford English Dictionary defines theme as "the subject of a piece of writing." I know that because I first looked it up when I began to write. Only problem is... that definition didn't do a whole lot in helping me understand what a theme actually is.

My first novel, *The Nowhere Man,* is about a decorated Navy SEAL, Kent Taylor, who becomes known as the "Ghost Assassin." But, the book isn't simply about a formidable man who uses his unique training and skills to assassinate people. It's about the man, himself, and what happens when you strip someone of everything and everyone he loves and trusts. We encounter a man who has no one he can turn to when he realizes the truth about the murders of his wife, his young son, and his in-laws by people in power in the very government he has risked his life for, time and again. Just as he would respond on a covert mission, Kent Taylor assumes the responsibility to take action against the people who were directly and indirectly responsible.

After reading this book, someone, who told me how much he enjoyed it, asked me why I didn't entitle the book, *The Ghost Assassin.* My answer was simple. The theme of this book was not to glorify the murders nor even the incredible skills displayed by my protagonist. The theme was to portray the utter emptiness a man is left with when what matters most in his life is unjustly taken away and he knows of no one he can trust for the justice he is seeking.

As a side note, many interviewers would ask me if I, especially being an attorney, believe that revenge killings are ever justifiable. I have answered, "No, they are never justifiable, but, sometimes, they are understandable."

In addition to providing entertainment, my novel leaves people with something to ponder and think about. It possesses a theme.

Some theme questions:

> Have I introduced a theme without being to "preachy" in my approach?

> Does my novel provoke readers to think beyond the book itself?

Vincent J. Sachar

Chapter Six

SOME WRITING TECHNIQUES

H OOK 'EM – As we mentioned earlier, the first chapter of your book needs to contain a *hook* that grabs a reader's attention and makes them want to continue reading. When I began writing my first murder mystery/thriller, I could hardly wait to introduce my new protagonist—Heather Lance, a twenty-four-year old female detective. This was also the first time I would be writing a novel where my primary character would be a female.

I began: "Heather Lance was driving much too fast for the winding, twisting mountain road on which she was driving." Not a terrible start, but this book is a mystery novel, a "who-dun-it" mystery/thriller. I went back and added a hook. My reader would be expecting a lead-in that this story will contain some hidden, mysterious happenings.

She turned off the engine and stepped out from her car. The night was black, overcast, devoid of any moonlight. A cool breeze pressed against her face and body and added to the chill that enveloped her. It was so dark—much too dark to actually see anyone—but he was there. She knew that he was. She could feel his presence. He had been there every night over the past few days. She anticipated before she even arrived back home that he would be somewhere, blended into the night's shadows, waiting for her.

Before Allison Martin drove away from the club, she watched, looking to see if anyone followed her out of the parking lot. She saw no one. She constantly checked the rear-view mirror as she drove along Mountain Highway, watching to see if at some point a car pulled out from behind her. No one followed her all the way home. He must have already been here, awaiting her arrival. Did he know her work schedule? Was he that aware of her?

Her body trembled as she walked slowly from her car to the front door. Why had she forgotten once again to leave the front light on? Stupid. Or had she turned it on before she headed off to work? She might have. She would have. She must have. She just could not remember. Besides, what did it matter now? She was walking in the darkness, not even able to see her feet touching the ground. And he was there. Somewhere.

She did not know who. She did not know where. She could not explain why. She only knew that he was there again tonight. And she could not think of any good reason why he would be.

Can you see it? Feel it? Did what I placed before my intro of Heather maybe put a little chill up your spine? Or get you to maybe think, "Hey, this is going to be exciting. I'm in." It honestly doesn't matter whether you're a writer, a public speaker, a singer, an actor, or a comedian. Anyone who is presenting something to a public audience has a very limited initial time before you either win over or lose your audience.

SHOW vs. TELL- One basic rule that authors will confront is the need to show and not merely tell when writing fiction. Before I provide further description of *showing* and *telling* and explain why showing is normally better than telling, let me begin with this caveat. This is not an absolute rule. Telling is not always wrong. As authors, our goal is to provide a balance between the two.

Okay, so what is *telling*? What is *showing*?

> **Telling** – Narrative. States a fact. Dictates a conclusion. Tells the reader what to think, feel, or believe.

> **Showing** – Permits the reader to experience for themselves, through the perspective of the characters.

Why is Showing Normally Preferred:

1. **Showing is More Entertaining** – Watching a movie or sports event is more entertaining than having someone tell you about it. And, the primary purpose of a fiction novel, for example, is to entertain the reader.

2. **Showing Respects the Intelligence of a Reader**- An author never wants to confuse the reader, but there is a level of trust and respect that can and should be extended to readers. When a writer takes the time to show, rather than tell, a reader is placed in position to rely upon their own intelligence and imagination.

   > "Sheila was exhausted as she pulled her car into the drveway." (Telling)

   > or

   > "Sheila pulled her car into the driveway and did not budge. She left the seatbelt fastened and threw her head back. Her breathing was reduced to panting. Her legs were like jelly. The distance to the front door of her home seemed miles away." (Showing)

3. **Showing Evokes More Emotions** – Generates a vicarious experience.

4. **Showing Draws Your Reader into the Story** – The reader is not merely watching something, they are participating. A reader can see, hear, smell,

touch, taste whatever is occurring. Showing triggers a reader's mind and imagination.

Signs You Might Be Telling and Not Showing:

1. Citing or Naming Emotions

Jack was angry. **(Telling)**

Jack bolted upright from his chair. His face was red, his eyes glowered at Fred. He slammed his fist on the table causing the coffee cup to tumble onto the ceramic tile floor and shatter. **(Showing)**

In the first example, the reader is simply told that a character is angry. In the second example, the reader is given an opportunity to draw a conclusion from what they might see or hear. Perhaps, the reader can see Jack suddenly on his feet with a reddened face and eyes glaring across the table. The reader might see Jack slam the table and hear the sound when his fist lands. In this example, a reader might picture the cup tumbling to the floor and see and hear it shattering.

In my novel, *The Nowhere Man*: Kent Taylor returns home from a covert mission as a Navy SEAL and discovers that his wife is dead from what is cited as an accidental house fire. Kent makes the painful visit to the house where his wife died.

"Kent was distraught as he stared at the two wine glasses from their wedding day. They drank from them yearly on each anniversary." **(Telling)**

"Kent spotted the wine glasses from their wedding day that they drank from on each anniversary. He picked them up, heaved them across the room, and watched as they shattered against the wall. They no longer served a purpose." **(Showing)**

In the first example, the reader is told that Kent is distraught. In the second example, the reader is given an opportunity to draw that conclusion based upon what the reader visualizes and experiences. The reader can see Kent lift the glasses and hurl them across the room. You might hear the glasses shatter as they strike the wall. The yearly ritual on each wedding anniversary is no longer relevant.

2. Descriptive Dialogue Tags

The use of descriptive dialogue tags may evidence that the dialogue itself is weak. The only purpose of a tag is to identify who is speaking.

> WRONG: "No, I won't do it," Fred said angrily.

> RIGHT: Fred rose from his chair and headed towards the door. Before bolting out of the room, he turned back to face his boss and raised a fist in the air.

> "No, I won't do it," he said.

Dialogue tags have only one purpose and that is to inform the reader who is speaking. The best way to assure that a writer is not improperly using tags is to primarily rely upon, "said" as your tag. While it is true that in the example above, it required some additional verbiage to avoid using an adverb in a dialogue tag, it is, nevertheless, preferable to bring your reader into a scene. Don't tell them. Show them.

3. Use of Broad Adjectives

It was *cold* outside

An *old* house

A *big* man

A *scary* sound

Broad adjectives, such as those listed in the above examples, tell, rather than show. They do not invite the reader into the scene. Give your reader enough to visualize and interpret what you want them to experience, while adding the touches of their own imagination. Remember, a book is a movie that is playing within a reader's mind.

There are many more examples that will help distinguish between showing and telling and a number of excellent books on the subject. We need to remember, especially when writing fiction, that our goal is to draw the reader into the scene of our writing. Find a way to permit the reader to rely upon the use of their five senses (sight, smell, touch, hearing, taste). Trust your readers to be able to discern emotions based upon the actions and descriptions we provide.

The Five (5) Senses- Writing is enhanced when we utilize the five senses. Once again, this helps to bring the reader deeper into our story.

Sight- This is the most obvious and easiest sense to describe. It has been said that a book is a movie that takes place in the reader's mind. Using this sense provides a world of benefit to a reader, such as color, texture, scenes, landscapes, objects, people's faces, and so much more.

Smell- This sense is the most closely linked with memory. It's the most nostalgic sense. Useful to get a character to remember an event (a flashback) useful to the present story. In your own life, think about situations where you catch the scent of something and are drawn back to another time, place, or event. The sense of smell generates strong emotions.

Taste- There are four (4) primary areas of taste: sweet, bitter, salty, and sour. Once again, they can be utilized to pull the reader deeper into the story. Taste used mostly when characters are eating or kissing. But, consider a character tasting a hint of salt in the air when near the ocean.

Touch- This sense is different from the others in that it can involve a multitude of body parts, including hands, face, neck, lips, tongue, fingertips, and feet. It also can be a powerful expression when one character reaches out to touch another. Touch can be pleasurable (e.g., the coolness of a pillow on a warm summer night) or painful (e.g., a head-butt) or neither (used to help describe a person or place (e.g., a cold handshake).

Sound- This sense can be greatly utilized in that it constitutes an early warning system that a writer can use to lead to so much more in the story. Sound descriptions create drama with sudden impact or add to the overall perspective of a scene. Most scenes have some sound that can be added to enhance that scene.

Summary

There are incredible resources, many of them free, online to help someone enhance their skills as a writer. I take time every week to study some aspects of creative writing. As I stated, you do not need to have a Ph.D in English to succeed as an author, but it makes perfect sense that we would want to learn and grow as writers.

In the next chapter, we will discuss today's publishing options and the ability of someone to quickly and efficiently get their book online, available to be purchased throughout the United States and abroad.

But, you want to write the best book you can. Remember: when a reader picks up your book, it can be compared to a first impression or a first date. It can lead to much more or serve to assure that the first impression was negative or that first date also was your last date.

Chapter Seven

PUBLISHING

The digital revolution is far more significant than the invention of writing or even of printing.

—Douglas Engelbart

D ouglas Engelbart was an American engineer, inventor, and early computer and internet pioneer. He is renowned for his work on founding the field of human-computer reaction which resulted in the invention of the computer mouse, the development of hypertext, and network computers. His statement certainly merits our attention. Engelbart was referring to the fact that today anyone can self-publish and have an eBook instantly on Amazon's Kindle, Barnes & Noble's Nook, Kobo, iBooks, and Google Play—the five most prominent sites. Everything no longer depends upon the sanction of a literary agent or a publisher.

There are advantages and disadvantages to mainstream publishing and self-publishing. I will share some of these in this chapter. My goal here is not to attempt to persuade you to take one path or another. Besides, a number of authors, myself included, travel down both paths. Rather, my goal is to provide you with a perspective regarding what is involved in each of the major options.

Traditional Publishing – This road generally begins with an author identifying literary agents to contact about your book. This is the job of the author. You must start this process. Let me take a moment here to provide a brief outline of the process:

- Identify a literary agent to whom you can send a communication. You can simply Google literary agents interested in the genre of your book. There are listings of agents available online. Remember: the agent must be someone interested in the genre you are writing in and must be currently accepting unsolicited submissions;

- Follow the submission guidelines the agent has set forth on his or her website. Some agents will only initially accept a *Query Letter* (a short one-page letter that expresses the topic of your work, a short description of the plot, a short bio of the author). Others may initially accept a *Query Letter* plus the first three chapters (or some other number of chapters or pages) of your manuscript. Some may ask for a *Synopsis* (a short description consisting of one or two pages describing the main events or ideas in a book). Other than the *Query Letter*, all submissions to an agent should be double-spaced. RULE OF THUMB: In addition to impeccable grammar, NEVER send more than the agent has listed in his or her submission guidelines;

- It may be weeks or months before you ever hear again from the agent. In some instances, you will receive a communication in which the agent states that he or she is not willing to represent your book. In some instances, an agent will ask you to send something additional, indicating at least a preliminary interest in your book;

- If the agent agrees to represent you, you will enter into an agreement with that agent. At some point, the agent will shop your book with publishers.

NOTE: A rejection from an agent does not necessarily reflect upon the quality of your writing. It may simply be that the agent does not believe that he or she has a viable market in which to attempt to generate interest in what you have written.

Some notable authors who received rejections: J. K. Rolwing's first Harry Potter book was rejected by twelve publishers before Bloomsbury picked it up for a very nominal advance fee. Other "rejected" authors include: J.R.R. Tolkien, John Steinbeck, John Updike, Kurt Vonnegut, James Baldwin, and William Faulkner. After five years of continual rejection, Agatha Christie finally landed a publishing deal. Her book sales are now in excess of two billion dollars, surpassed only by William Shakespeare. Louis L'Amour received 200 rejections before Bantam offered a publishing agreement. He is now their best selling author ever with more than three hundred million sales.

We can go on-and-on citing examples of famous authors and works that were the subject of countless rejections.

If your book is accepted by a publisher, you will receive a Publisher/Author Agreement which sets forth the responsibilities and duties of the parties. Generally, the author agrees to submit copies of the mansucript to the publisher. The publisher will take responsibilty for editing, creating a book cover (generally this is a collaborative effort between the publisher and author), and publishing within a prescibed period of time. Royalty fees payable to the author are set forth for print books, digital or eBooks, and audio books. In some instances, you might be able to negotiate a bit on royalty fees, but, generally, especially for a newly-signed author, you will have to take what the publisher offers.

The publisher will establish some level of a marketing strategy which might include online interviews, book signings, the release of marketing materials, and things of this nature. The changes in the publishing landscape are such that publishers provide much less to an author than in times past and many publishers do not offer an advance fee.

Self-Publishing – The stigma that self-publishing is indicative of an author's inability to latch onto a publisher has been largely eradicated in today's publishing world. Many of today's top authors will self-publish in addition to works published traditionally. Self-publishing offers an author greater control over their product and more revenue. But, if you're going to self-publish, you need to do your homework. Find the reputable companies to deal with. Some of the more popular self-publishing platforms are: Amazon's CreateSpace, Lulu, Kindle Direct Publishing (for eBooks), Kobo, Blurb, Xlibris, BookBaby, and SmashWords.

Some questions to ask any company you are considering using:

1. Exclusive or Non-Exclusive – Most e-publishing services are non-exclusive, which means you can use their service to sell your books while also selling anywhere else you choose (A notable exception is Amazon's Kindle Direct which requires a three-month exclusive if you join the program. In return, your book can be lent out through Kindle Unlimited and the Kindle Owner's Lending Library.)

2. Who Controls the Price? – Standard practice is that the author controls the pricing. Amazon has a policy to automatically lower your book price if they find it cheaper anywhere else.

3. **What's the Upfront Fee? How is Royalty Calculated?** – Amazon KDP, Barnes & Noble's Nook Press, and Apple's iBookstore are all free to use. They make their money by taking a cut of your sales. Generally, you earn 60%-70% of your list price, provided your price is within certain specified ranges. Smashwords is free, distributes to all major eBook retailers except Amazon, and pays you 85% of sales directly through the Smashwords site minus PayPal transaction fees. With BookBaby, you can pay nothing upfront, get eBook formatting/conversion, and give them a percentage of your sales, or pay a flat fee up front and keep 100% of your net sales.

4. **What File Formats Do They Accept?** – Microsoft Word is commonly accepted. EPUB is the industry standard eBook format. You can find many conversion/formatting services online that offer EPUB and MOBI files that will cover you with Amazon and just about every other book retailer.

The top five (5) sites are: Amazon Kindle, Nook, Kobo, iBooks, and Google Play.

The primary challenges to self-publishing exist in the fact that you are assuming responsibility for editing your manuscript, for creating a book cover, and for all other aspects, such as formatting the text for submission to certain sites. Once again, if you take the time to do your homework, you can find many available sources that can assist you with these things and save you money in the process. Another key factor, and this also impacts upon your expenses, is whether you choose to self-publish an eBook only, a paperback only, or both. The least expensive road is self-publishing an eBook. In fact, some authors will publish the digital eBook first and follow up with a paperback, afterwards. I, personally, have all of my novels in both formats (paperback and eBook), but have limited the short stories and novellas to digital only.

Do not let any of this overwhelm you. It is not all that difficult at all to get your book self-published. But, take the time to do your homework. Once I self-published, my books are on sites worldwide and I have sales in both Europe and Asia, as well as throughout the United States.

Some Things to Remember:

1. Whether you desire to publish through a traditional publisher and the process of finding a literary agent to place your book with a publisher or whether you desire to self-publish, you need to take time to do your homework. There's a plethora of info available on the Internet. Take the time to explore the facets of traditional publishing and self-publishing so that you are in the best position to make choices and to do things correctly;

2. Nothing is more important than to write the best book that you can. In such a competitive field, you can only count on getting one opportunity to make that positive first impression as a writer;

3. Determine whether you will only publish an eBook or a print book, also. You can publish an eBook first and wait to do a print book afterwards;

4. Explore the companies that can help you self-publish: CreateSpace (owned by Amazon), Barnes & Noble's Nookpress, Lulu, iUniverse, Llumina, xlibris, outskirts press. Research them. Look for *a la carte* service items (e.g., perhaps you can acquire a quality book cover cheaper somewhere else, rather than pay one of these companies and their graphic artists to create one).

6. Some Common Questions:

- What is an ISBN and do I need one?

  ISBN stands for International Standard Book Number which is a unique identifier of books. Any book made publicly available for sale can be identified by its ISBN. It is mandatory for all print books. Amazon's Kindle does not require an ISBN for eBooks. Apple's iBookstore does require an ISBN for each title you intend to sell. Other sites have their own requirements. In the United States, you can only obtain an ISBN through the Bowker company. (myidentifiers.com then click on "ISBN Identifiers") Better to buy in bulk. One ISBN, for example, costs $125. Ten ISBNs cost $250.

- *If I publish a paperback, will I get stuck with a bunch of books collecting dust on a shelf somewhere that I have to pay for?*

No, thanks to POD, which stands for "Print On Demand." When one of your books is ordered online, the book is then printed and mailed out.

- *Do I need to file for copyright protection with the U.S. Copyright Office?*

No. Your work is protected by copyright the moment you write or create it. Filing for additional copyright protection with the U.S. Copyright Office is not needed unless you desire extra protection in a possible lawsuit.

- *What are key elements to consider when creating my book?*

Whether your book is a print book or an eBook only, consider that the first thing a potential reader does is look at the cover. Covers should be bright, bold, with the title in upper case contrasting color. Covers should depict the theme or tone of your book. Consider your title and the message it sends to a reader. Once a person gets past your cover and is still somewhat interested, remember that the back cover blurb is crucial to stimulating interest in that potential reader. If you are not comfortable enough in creating this, shop online for someone who can assist you. But, above all else, strive to write the very best book you can. Your storyline needs to be interesting and connected. Eliminate sloppiness. Make sure you provide closure on any open questions that exist. Be sure to develop a strong beginning and ending to your book. The opening chapters draw the reader in. No one is going to read a book with a weak, fizzled ending and be satisfied that this was a good read.

- *Is it better to wait for a traditional publisher or self-publish?*

  There are advantages to both, but the process in getting a publisher to take your book is a much slower and demanding route. If you are going to seek the traditional route, you will need to know how to write a *Query Letter* for submission to literary agents. You'll have to familiarize yourself with how to write a *Synopsis,* in some instances. Do your research. Take some time to consider your options, while you write the best book that you can.

- *Should I create an author website?*

  Yes, give people a place to go to in order to learn more about you and your writings. There are many different website builders available on the market that offer a range of features. If you're a beginner, the thought of designing your own website can be overwhelming (I felt this at first), but it need not be. Most sites will lead you through the process in a seamless manner. (WiX.com; web.com; sitebuilder.com; weebly; eHost.com).

- *Where do I find the resources to help me as a writer and in my desire to publish?*

Think of it this way. The moment something new arises, a whole bunch of small, supplementary businesses and resources come to life. For every need you may have as an author who wants to be published, there is someone out there poised to assist you. There are many free resources online that can teach you much. There are eBooks galore on virtually every subject you want to know more about available at inexpensive prices. Trust me. You can find the answers and even acquire assistance for every need you have. And, you will often save quite a bit of money by searching for and exploring the opportunities available to you. Stop biting your nails, convincing yourself this is too difficult, and get to work. You'll be shocked at just how much is available to you.

- *What about having my books available at retail bookstores like Barnes & Noble or Books-A-Million?*

You can submit copies of your books to the American Wholesale Book Company for Books-A-Million or to Barnes & Noble for approval of your books to be sold through their stores. The prospect of having my books scrunched in among so many books on shelves has limited value to me. However, you can be in position where anyone can enter one of these retail stores and order your books. Today's consumer often shops online and makes their purchases that way, so you'll need to decide for yourself just how important this is to you. Making my books available through Barnes & Noble, for example, has been of benefit for a number of book signings I have done at their retail stores. This is based upon the fact that a Barnes & Noble store orders in your books itself for an event. You are prohibited from bringing in your own supply of books. Once again, however, I have found that the number of books you sell at these events can be quite limited.

Chapter Eight

SUMMARY

The primary purpose of *For the Writer in You* is to encourage you to live out your dream of writing a book and becoming a published author. There is so much more that we could discuss herein, but I hope that I have at least given you much to think about. If we would summarize what we have been saying, here are some key points:

- Writing is your personal responsibility. No one can do it for you (unless you hire a ghostwriter and even then the basis of your novel is inside your own head). There's a discipline required, without which nothing more will happen. And it's never too late to start. *The best time to plant a tree was twenty years ago. The next best time is now.*

- Every author should take some time each week to search out and study writing techniques. You can find so much online or even acquire some inexpensive books that touch upon various subjects that are helpful to an author.

- In your quest, set goals, not expectations. Goals are things you have control over and can achieve (e.g.,

I will finish my book within this time range. I will do at least some writing every day.) Expectations are things over which you have no control and failure to reach them can lead to discouragement (I will be a New York Times Bestseller. I will sell 10,000 books in my first month after launching my novel).

- Strive to write the best book you can. Remember that the number one purpose of a fiction novel is to entertain the reader. The primary purpose of a non-fiction book is to explain or inform. No, you do not have to have a Ph.D in English to be an author, but you certainly should strive to be fundamentally sound with your grammar and spelling. Take the time to polish up on things and learn some basic rules. (In the United States, punctuation is placed inside quotation marks. The opposite is true in the United Kingdom. Generally, for numbers zero through one hundred, spell out the number (e.g., thirty).

- Explore today's publishing landscape. The options available to you are greater than ever before in history. Search for reputable service providers. Stay away from the scammers. Even when you are dealing with a reputable company, you still have options. Inquire about *a la carte* pricing. How much for a book cover? Perhaps, I can get that work done cheaper elsewhere and just submit my cover. How much for interior formatting and design? Go through the items and find the best deal for yourself. Believe me, it sounds more complicated than it is. If your budget is tight, consider starting with an eBook only and working towards a print book afterwards. There's a digital revolution occurring today. Get on board.

- Remember: you don't have to write a book today. But, if this is a dream you have, you can begin, even now, to move in that direction. Take some time to study aspects of creative writing. Learn more, at your own pace, about the publishing options available to you. You might consider keeping a journal to jot down story ideas as they pop into your head. Have some fun creating characters. Name them. Describe them. Let your imagination flow. These things will help to keep your dreams alive.

- And remember: Choose to believe in yourself. If you don't believe in you, no one else will.

www.ingramcontent.com/pod-product-compliance
Lightning Source LLC
Chambersburg PA
CBHW060657030426

42337CB00017B/2667